BAƧIC
FRAΛK LLOYD WRIGHT

**Legend and Fact
About America's
Most Creative
Architect**

Henry J. Michel

ONE PALM BOOKS
Los Angeles , California

BASIC FRANK LLOYD WRIGHT
Legend and Fact About
America's Most Creative Architect

Copy editing by D. A. Wetterberg

Book and cover design
by Andy Chase

Library of Congress Card Number 99-70549
ISBN 0-9652237-2-8

Printed in U. S. A.

ONE PALM BOOKS is an imprint of
Michel Publishing Services
4842 Tilden Ave. Sherman Oaks, CA 91423

PREFATORY COMMENTS

a.	Why This Book Was Written

In over seven years serving as a volunteer docent at houses designed by Frank Lloyd Wright, I've heard some strange questions asked by visitors and have also heard many inaccurate stories told about the architect.

Frequently I heard statements attributing structures to Wright that he had nothing to do with and even more frequently I saw that many persons who had some knowledge of Wright's life were unaware of some of his greatest works.

This showed me clearly that among the general public there is quite a bit of these two things: misinformation, and lack of information. That's not surprising, except that there are literally tons of information on Wright. On the internet one bookseller's catalog lists over 100 Wright books.

The trouble is that most of these have been written by architecturally trained or expert people writing mostly for a similarly leaning audience, whether professionals or knowledgeable art enthusiasts.

This book is an alternative source for those who desire a short, compact rendition of the significant events in Wright's life and a non-technical account of his major works and how they came about.

b.   What This Book Contains

Misinformation was mentioned above. This book will do little to change that situation. In fact, it will continue to pass on some of the tales the legendary Wright is made of - some myths, some half-truths, some doubtful and not-well- documented facts about the man and his life. It is partly the stuff that makes Wright a bigger-than-life character.

But as to lack of information, the second problem mentioned, this book offers to those who would spend a bit of time with it, a quick overview of the architect's life and his work. For some readers this will be sufficient. Others may be driven to delve into more details elsewhere.

It is hoped this book will encourage you to rise from your chair and visit the closest Frank Lloyd Wright-designed building. If you are so moved and just don't know where to go, look at the short list of sites at the back of the book. It may be the start of a life-long interest.

c.   How I Had The Nerve To Write This Book

I am not an architect. Nor am I an engineer or designer of any sort. Like the majority of those who will read this book - and for whom it was primarily written - I an not trained in any of the arts related to architecture. So, why did I have the nerve to attempt this book? Here is my excuse.

I once knew very little about Frank Lloyd Wright. This in spite of growing up not far from his original Oak Park, Illinois home and studio and often cycling or driving on those streets where many of his early works were built. I knew little about the architect until years later.
In the last decade that has changed. I am now an expert amateur - or is it an amateur expert? Either designation,

you'll agree, hints that I don't know everything, or perhaps that some of what I know may not be fact. On the other hand, no one can be sure that everything written about Wright is indeed fact. Experts (the professional kind) who write about him often differ in their writings about him.

Many books on Wright are aimed at an esoteric audience, versed in art or architecture. But what about - I dislike the term, but it is useful - *the average person?* Shouldn't there be a book intended primarily for that vast group? The logical answer is "yes."

That being the case, I thought it would serve a good purpose to assemble a sketch of his life. It would be useful to those who find themselves as I (being an average person) once was; knowing not much about Wright. And it may serve even those who know somewhat more.

My qualifications for this are that I served for several years as docent or interpreter at several Frank Lloyd Wright houses and have also compiled and published two useful guidebooks to Wright's works in California and Arizona.

After this book, I recommend you read some of the many books on Wright available at your library or bookstore. Before you know it you will be considering yourself an "Expert Amateur."

H.J.M.

Sprite
(salvage), **Midway Gardens**, Chicago, 1903

CONTENTS

early period, **Blossom House**, Chicago, 1892

A CAREER BEGINS

I start this story of the architect's life when he was twenty and will pick up the earlier years later. First you will see how the young Frank Lloyd Wright rose to success and wide fame before he even reached the mid-point of his life. This was achieved within the relatively short time of twenty two years.

If this strikes you as being quite a long time for a career to come to fruition, consider this: the first quarter of those years were years of learning and then transitioning into a personal style, because Wright had had little formal schooling in the arts or the sciences that comprise the profession of architecture. The young Wright had only some incidental involvements with design and construction when he decided to leave his then Madison, Wisconsin home to seek his fortune in the big city as an architect in Chicago.

The results of his next two decades seem all the more unexpected when, as it appears, there was little in his childhood pointing to such an eventual burst of genius. From what is known, Wright's often-interrupted schooling was not marked with anything spectacular. His family moved repeatedly during his young years which may have blunted his liking for formal schooling. It seems he was at best an average student, with no particular driving interests.

It is probably a good thing that in those days architectural studies *per se* were generally non-existent in colleges and universities, except at a few eastern schools. It's unlikely that Wright could have adapted well to any formalized course of study as it would have been presented then. Both the professors and Wright might have suffered bouts of severe frustration. Too much of an individualist, he probably would have aborted the academic approach.

As things were, however, those who wanted to pursue the profession could learn it as apprentices to practicing architects. Of course, starting as an apprentice did not immediately involve designing buildings. A novice might first do plan tracing, work up to drafting, and then become an architect's assistant, doing design work and construction supervision. Wright entered the profession in this routine way but he rose with anything but routine speed.

After a few months working under an architect whose style was not much to Wright's liking, he was fortunate to be taken on by one of the most talented architects working in Chicago, Louis H. Sullivan. In the next few years, the firm of Adler and Sullivan would produce some of the most architecturally advanced structures in the city, or anywhere else for that matter. Chicago was the birthplace of the steel-framed *skyscraper*, and Adler and Sullivan was one of its midwives.

In just two years Wright became the head draftsman

of the firm, working directly under Sullivan and supervising the entire drafting staff. The two became close - mentor and protégé - with Sullivan assuming status of a father-figure for the then fatherless Wright.

Even as draftsman, Wright became well-known locally in the profession. Daniel H. Burnham, the most prominent and successful architect in the city, approached Wright with an offer to pay his way (all expenses, family included) for four years at the Ecole de Beaux Arts in Paris (a school in the classical traditions) and guaranteeing Wright a job in his firm upon his return. Wright declined the offer.

Adler and Sullivan specialized in larger public buildings. One of its greatest successes is the Auditorium Building which still stands on Michigan Avenue in Chicago. As the first multi-use building, it was designed as a hotel, office building, and theater. When finished, the firm took space at the top of its office tower, at that time the tallest structure in the city. For many years now the building has housed Roosevelt University. The theater still mounts live productions.

When the firm occasionally did a residential design as an accommodation to major clients or friends, the designing was assigned to a senior draftsman such as Wright. The very interesting Charnley house, still existing on Astor Street in the near north side of the city, is one of Wright's projects done for the firm.

But residences done in the name of the firm were not the only houses that issued forth at the beginning of Wright's career. He was now married with a growing family and a growing appetite for the finer things in life.

Also growing was the new suburb of Oak Park west of Chicago where Wright lived, and he was helping it grow. He was designing and building homes for his private clients in violation of his contract with Adler and Sullivan. Not only did he build in his own neighborhood but (and this seems a foolhardy move), virtually under his employer's nose in the then fashionable South Lakeshore district where Sullivan lived.

How much Sullivan knew of Wright's moonlighting and when did he know it are matters sometimes discussed by historians. In any event, Sullivan finally confronted Wright with this violation of his contract and - whether he had first intended to or not - the fiery Sullivan fired Wright.

Wright's departure may have been inevitable in any case. Now he was able to get out on his own and begin what would culminated in the next dozen years in a style and body of work so distinct as to have its own name: *Prairie House.* Later on there even emerged a so-called Prairie school of architects who copied or incorporated much of the style that Wright had created into their own work. In 1893, his first year on his own, Frank Lloyd Wright, Architect secured half a dozen commissions.

The Prairie House did not blossom immediately. Like his "bootleg" houses, as he called his moonlighting efforts, Wright's first commissions were executed in various existing and popular styles ranging from Queen Anne to Tudor half-timber - but most of them with variations here and there that foreshadowed the elements that would later predominate in his full-blown *Prairie* designs.

early period, **Moore House**, Oak Park, IL 1895
(upper floors rebuilt after 1922 fire)

A Prairie House
Robie House, Chicago, 1906

In what came to be called his *Prairie* houses, Wright eliminated all of the curlicues, "gingerbread" and lavish ornament so typical in the houses of the period. He avoided parroting current styles derived from their classical ancestors. The *Prairie House* hugged its site under a low-pitched hip roof that spread over wide eaves. Long bands of windows opened the house to the outside and added to its horizontal lines. He eschewed attics and deep basements, and did away with walls between the public rooms - "destroying the boxes," as he described it.

But Wright would build a considerable number of houses and a few larger structures before creating what most historians regard as the first true delineation of the Prairie style house, the Willetts residence in Highland Park, Illinois. This was at the turn of the century, 1901, and that style predominated his output for the next ten years. The *Prairie House* brought Frank Lloyd Wright to national and international attention. The name grew out of an illustrated article published that year in *Ladies Home Journal* magazine titled "A Home in a Prairie Town."

There were some non-residential buildings completed as well and two in particular added to his celebrity, especially in the architectural community. The Larkin Company administration building in Buffalo, N.Y. was an unconventional office building that included not only numerous inventions of his but also experimental concepts in workplace design.

At about the same time, at home in Oak Park, Wright was constructing Unity Temple. It too was unconventional like the Larkin building, more so, perhaps, in

that it was a church built of poured, reinforced concrete. The severe-looking square structure might lead
the uninformed to take it to be a library or a court-
house. Whatever one was to take it for, they might also
wonder how anyone gets into the place? One of the
"tricks" Wright often used in both residential and public
buildings was to design an unobtrusive entrance,
thereby conferring a greater degree of privacy to the
building. While the Larkin building is long gone, Unity
Temple still functions and can be visited most after-
noons.

By the end of the decade Wright had become known
to a large segment of the public and to all in the art
world. He also became controversial in architectural
circles. Displaying his "honest arrogance" (which he
said he adopted over "hypocritical humility"), he made
it appear that he cared little about his critic's lack of
appreciation of his work. And he showed he cared
even less for what he regarded as their unimaginative
designs. He scolded the establishment and challenged
them to design better homes - and better cities. He
never joined any professional group.

In the fall of 1909 he brought an abrupt end not only
to the creation of his *Prairie Houses* but to his career
as it stood at the time. He shut down his studio and left
his unfinished projects to be completed by another
architect. He went to Europe for an entire year,
ostensibly for the purpose of preparing a monograph
of his work for a German publisher. But there was a lot
more to it than that, as you shall see later.

2

BIRTH TO MID-LIFE CRISIS

Given the facts in the previous section, anyone with a bit of curiosity might well wonder what sort of life Wright had in his formative years and - perhaps more so - what was the nature of his personal life during those two decades in which he became such a prominent figure in American architecture. In this section you get an overview of his life in those two time periods.

Anna Lloyd Jones, his mother, was of that Welsh clan of Lloyd Joneses that in mid-century immigrated from Wales to the Helena Valley near Spring Green, Wisconsin, where in 1867 Wright was born in the small burg of Richland Center. Wright's maternal kin were more actively involved with him in his childhood than as an adult.   Yet, he established Taliesin, his second home, in the *"valley of the Lloyd Joneses"* where he was born, which may indicate his continuing attachment to his heritage and to his maternal family.

Being Unitarians meant the Lloyd Joneses were a minority and this undoubtedly contributed to their decision to leave Britain. They were hard working, frugal, clannish, fairly well educated for the times, and given to a variety of talents. They were farmers, teachers and ministers - and as a group, religious.

Eventually, their descendants spread a wealth of various talents across the land. In addition to Frank, whose work literally spanned the country east to west and border to border, other progeny of these immigrant Welsh became prominent in fields as diverse as publishing, law and the theater. In fact, there were others who ventured into architecture.

As a young boy, Frank learned to dislike farm work to which he was exposed during long, tiring summers working with his uncles. Later, as a young man in Chicago, he would still be under the eye of his uncle, a prominent minister who headed a large church there. But it was his mother who for better or for worse would have a most direct and lasting influence over him until her death.

His father, William Carey Wright, was from New England and of English descent; thus an outsider as regards the clan. His father was a Baptist minister. William was well educated and naturally talented for many skills - music and oratory among them. A widower with three children, he married Anna who was a good deal younger than he was. She never fully accepted his first family. His children soon went to live with other relatives.

Although trained to some degree in both medicine and law, William chose to follow the ministry, first as a Baptist, later changing to Unitarian. As a New Englander he had sided with the North in the recent Civil War and was an avid admirer of Lincoln - an attitude also prevalent among the Lloyd Joneses. It is not surprising, then, that when Frank was born two years after Lincoln's assassination, the boy was christened Frank Lincoln Wright.

William Wright's second family eventually included Frank and two younger sisters. He moved the family to New England where they lived in several towns as he took positions in various churches. William was well liked by his parishioners as well as the other towns-people everywhere he went. The congregations, however, were not affluent and his ministry income was small requiring him to supplement it through his music and lecturing. This meager hand-to-mouth living eventually wore thin with Anna. The family returned to Wisconsin, where William again struggled trying to manage several occupations simultaneously to gain a better livelihood.

Eventually the growing friction between William and Anna came to a head. Unlikely as it might seem for those times, especially in the case of a minister, William left his wife, all but driven out of the house. Frank was in his late teens when his father, under an agreement sanctioned by Frank's uncles, left the Madison house to Anna and the children and went off to secure a divorce.

Frank never saw or spoke to his father after that. As if in defiant anger and as a sign that he now belonged solely to the Lloyd Joneses, Frank substituted the name Lloyd for Lincoln and, in the manner followed by many in his maternal family, he would actively use that name as a part of his.

Frank was still of high school age when his father left but no evidence has been found that he completed high school. Yet he was able to take some courses at the University of Wisconsin as an unmatriculated student. This may have been through the aegis of his employer, a contractor who was also the dean of the school's engineering department. In two terms he took several courses including some engineering subjects. Then, approaching the age of twenty, it is said, he secretly pawned some books and other items to fund his "escape," and off he went to Chicago, intent on becoming an architect.

Having progressed to this point in the story, you may be wondering when you will encounter one of those myths or legends referred to in the introductory section. This is as good a place as any. There is the oft-told story that is certainly legendary now, but I leave it to you to classify fact or fiction. It comes from Wright's own autobiography which is regarded by many as containing a bit of hyperbole and even some outright nonsense.

It is said that his mother, Anna, while carrying her child literally willed the fetus in her womb to be a builder. And to buffer her prenatal projection, she festooned his various infant and childhood sleeping quarters with etchings of classical buildings to engender and reinforce in the youth the appreciation of such art.

When the boy was older, as another legend goes, Anna secured for him a set of the Friedrich Froeble toys (or "gifts" as the German exponent of child develbpm entm ethods and coinerofthe term *kinder-garten* referred to them), having seen them at the

Philadelphia Exposition of 1876. Wright relates that he recalls playing with those blocks and other materials designed to give a child an appreciation of shape, texture, color and other tactile and visual properties. You can seek more details in some of the many books on Wright's life. In this brief. book, however, I will proceed with more highlights of his personal and professional life.

Shortly after arriving in Chicago, young Frank secured his first job with Joseph Silsbee, a popular architect who had done several projects for Frank's minister-uncle, including a small family chapel in the Lloyd Joneses' valley in Wisconsin. Frank had given some assistance in the construction of the little chapel and had actually designed some of the interior features. Now he played on this earlier acquaintanceship and Silsbee took him on as a tracer, first at eight dollars a week, then upping it to twelve. When Silsby balked at a second raise, Wright left and obtained another job at fifteen dollars. But the job was beyond him. He had gotten in over his head. So he returned to Silsby and evidencing his new salary as a measure of his worth, was taken back by his first employer at the higher rate.

A few months later his career really made a significant advance when he switched to the firm of Adler and Sullivan. Not only did his professional achievements begin to grow, so did his social skills and appetites.

The young provincial Wisconsin lad quickly adjusted to the faster, more active pace of life in Chicago. Frank socialized with some of the young professionals who were also establishing their careers in the dynamic

commercial world taking shape in this city that was
continuing its rebuilding and growth after the devastating fire of 1871. Wright took to wearing fashionable
clothes, he developed a taste for the theatre, concerts
and ballet, and he joined men's social clubs and
attended social events organized by his uncle's
church. It was at a church costume party, in a minor
mishap on the dance floor, that Frank literally ran into
his future wife, Catherine Tobin.

He had taken particular notice of Catherine on other
occasions but had not formally met her. This acciden-
tal encounter eliminated the need for formality and the
pair struck up an immediate friendship. Frank carried
on a courtship for several months that lead to a young
love affair and, in an inordinately short time, there was
talk of marriage.

Catherine came from a fairly prosperous family. She
was educated but young and immature, exactly what
mother Anna feared most would happen to her Frank
- although any other female would have been the
same in Anna's mind.

 As Frank continued his courtship, the girl's parents,
because of her age, also resisted when talk of
marriage came up. Despite a forced separation, with
Catherine sent to visit distant relatives, the romance
continued and in June of 1889 Frank and Catherine
were married. She was eighteen, Frank would be
twenty-two the following week.

No longer the bachelor, Wright now realized that with a
wife and the prospects of a growing family he had
better establish a suitable home. No doubt he had

confidence in his ability to progress in his career and in a secure position in the firm. He took advantage of his closeness with Sullivan and asked him for a loan to purchase a plot and build a house for himself and Catherine. This was arranged, Sullivan holding the mortgage deed on the property in Oak Park where Wright had selected a large lot at the corner of Chicago and Forest Avenues. The house was placed on the south portion of the lot, leaving considerable space along the Chicago Avenue frontage, where some years later Wright would build his studio, connecting it directly to the house.

The house itself was a far cry from what would later bring the architect to the attention of the country. It was in a style closer to what his first employer, Silsby, might have designed. The small two-bedroom house would undergo continual changes and expansion over the years. This would include not only the eventual adjacent studio, but a cavernous play room with a high barrel-vault ceiling. All of this can now be seen on one of the guided tours offered daily by the Frank Lloyd Wright Foundation.

The Wrights grew in number. The first offspring was a male and appropriately named after his father. Although technically *Frank Jr.,* he was called Lloyd, by his family and he continued to use Lloyd Wright throughout his life and career as an architect, to differentiate his name from his father's famous moniker. The second child, also a boy, was named John Lloyd, and he was followed by four other children, two boys and two girls. Of these, only John was to also involve himself in architecture. At different times both older boys worked with their father on various projects.

Of the two architect sons, it was Lloyd who had the more prominent career, much of his work being done in California and the West.

This rather large family was not untypical of families of the time, nor of those in the fast-blooming suburb of Oak Park. The Wrights became in many ways like that new breed of Americans cropping up around the major industrial and commercial cities around the country: *Suburbanites.* Catherine participated in social and civic activities of the town. They were members, but not necessarily regular attendant ones, of the Unitarian church a few blocks from their home, the church that burned and that Wright received the commission to rebuild: his famous Unity Temple.

Frank belonged to several community clubs and organizations. He rode horseback, belonged to the country club, attended theatrical and musical performances locally and in the city. He also was a pain in the neck to some of the neighbors. The children were somewhat undisciplined, or so the neighbors thought (propriety then being one of the hallmarks of suburban life). They may have been right, since Frank did not involve himself with child rearing. That was Catherine's realm. And then there was Frank's automobile, or more specifically, his driving.

With a great attraction to things mechanical, it's not surprising that Wright owned one of the first three automobiles in Oak Park. The little open two-seater that neighbors dubbed *the Yellow Devil,* frequently sped noisily on the otherwise quiet streets of the town, and its driver acquired more than a few citations for infractions of the law. His love of the motor car never diminished and later, when he could afford it, (and often when he couldn't) he indulged himself in larger and more expensive lines, like Packard and Lincoln, sometimes having them repainted in his favorite color, Cherokee red.

While an inordinate attachment to the automobile was not an uncommon thing among many men of that period, (and for time ever after, for that matter) there were other more distinctive characteristics that became a part of Wright's makeup and demeanor. One idiosyncrasy, purposefully displayed by him, was the unorthodox attire he increasingly adopted in the years after he began his independent practice .

In his first years working as a young draftsman, newly arrived In the big city Frank quickly boaomo an exponent of the fashionable styles of the time. In his early but brief man-about-town period he appears to have matched his fellow young Turks in their fashionable sartorial styles. A frequently published photo of that period shows him and a friend and coworker dressed almost identically.

Later on, however, Wright embraces many unconventional affectations in his dress. The broad-rimmed, flat-crowned hat and cape are seen in many photographs and films of the architect. The walking stick lent a sort of authoritarian air to his confident swagger. But there were other, less obvious variants from the styles of the day. Billowy cravats, velvet trousers, ruffle-trimmed shirts were just some of the items that made his wardrobe lean more to costume than elegant attire. In a letter written by his Oak Park friend, Wm. E. Martin, who agreed to drive Wright to the rail depot to claim his luggage upon return from Europe, Martin tells his brother that Wright "was dressed to closely resemble the man on the Quaker Oats package."

This flair for the theatrical remained a facet of Wright's personality and life. His costumes seemed to fit with many of his unorthodox actions and most certainly were intended to reinforce the idea that he was not just an architect but an artist in the fullest sense of the word.

While these overt displays may drive some biographers to venture into psychological analysis, there is no space here to discuss the whys and wherefors. It is best to move on to point out some of the other characteristics that made Wright's personality as unconventional and interesting as some of his works. According to what is written by those who studied his life in detail, Wright had many flaws that related to his use and misuse of money.

He was an uncontrollable spendthrift. He spent for himself at times when money was in his hand, and often when no money was at hand. He ran up bills, not only on the necessities of his household, but on things that struck his fancy, even while debts remained unpaid. His poor credit status was well known among the merchants of Oak Park. One can only wonder why they continued to extend it so liberally. There is one story of a sheriff camping at his house while Wright scrambled to scrounge up the money to satisfy a creditor.

These debts arising from household or personal

expenditures were "small potatoes" compared to his frequent borrowings from friends - often his past clients - who, like the local merchants, repeatedly succumbed to Wright's charm in his appeals with loans on virtually no collateral. These financial difficulties were ever present during the greater part of his life, when his irregular and uncertain income seldom met the outflow. Only in the last quarter of his life was he able to afford to live in the style he desired.

Aside from his economic problems, Wright had another character trait that dominated his personality: his ego. He took a very subjective view of the Lloyd Jones clan's family motto *"Truth Against the World"* and seemed to believe it meant *his* truth. The literature is full of examples where he insists that he is right and others are not. One can see his defiance exhibited in both his work and in his personal life.

In the second decade of his independent career, he continued to build a reputation that evoked admiration by many and criticism by some. He basked in the admiration and continued to strike back with invectiveness at the *establishments*, both in architecture and in society in general.

After a marriage of some twenty years and six children, Wright tired of his domestic roll. His relationship with Catherine was strained. His mid-life crisis went into full bloom when he took up with the wife of a former Oak Park client, Mamah Borthwick Cheney. The illicit affair started to simmer locally, but it boiled over into a grand scandal that played out from Chicago to Europe.

In the fall of 1909 Wright left his family and went to Europe for a year. He had been approached by a German publisher to produce a monograph of his designs and he used this opportunity to escape Oak Park, his family responsibilities, and the scandal growing out his affair with Mamah. She left her husband and her children and met Wright in New York and sailed away with him.

It was a soap opera-like year. She spent some of her time in Berlin, studying, writing and later teaching. He spent time around Florence, Italy, working on the book. He even brought over his son Lloyd to help him with the art work. Catherine faced floods of reporters at home, defended her husband against both friends and foes, and remained in denial, stating repeatedly that Wright would return to his family. She was partially right.

A year later Wright returned to Oak Park and was welcomed by his wife and children. Not quite so forgiving were the townspeople. Wright wrote about them in a letter to a friend stating he was used to some alienation before, but now the women of the town faced away and pulled their skirts aside as he passed on the street. His career in Oak Park was dead.

Wright decided to leave the unfriendly town and build a home and working quarters in the Wisconsin valley of his birth, on land his mother had acquired from one of his uncles. It was adjacent to Hillside Home School, a progressive co-educational boarding school run by his two maiden aunts. To the inquisitive Wright said he was building a home for his mother, but it soon took on obvious greater dimensions, and upon completion in 1911, the complex, with separate living quarters for Anna, became the principal home and studio for Wright. He gave it a Welsh name: *Taliesin.* To this bucolic hidden paradise on the banks of the Wisconsin River, he brought the now divorced Mamah Borthwick.

In the late summer of 1914, the two Cheney children, John and Martha were visiting their mother at Taliesin. (Mr. Cheney had been awarded permanent custody.) The mid-day meal had been served to them and their mother and six members of the Taliesin staff seated In the dining area and the adjacent screened-in porch. As they ate, the domestic servant who had served the meal locked all but one of the doors accessing those areas, then, using gasoline, ignited fires all around. The nine diners were trapped with but one exit.

As they tried to escape - some crashing through the porch screens, others through the only open door, the servant attacked them all with an ax. When the horrible incident ended, Mamah, her children, and four others lay dead or dying. A major part of Taliesin burned to the ground.

A Prairie House
May House, Grand Rapids, MI, 1908

JAPAN AND
THE MIDDLE YEARS

After Wright's return from Europe his output de-
creased for several reasons. The scandal undoubtedly
caused potential clients in the Chicago area to seek a
less controversial, or as some might regard: *notorious*,
person to design their abodes. Still, in the next five
years Wright executed several projects in Chicago
suburbs as well as some in other states. But the flow
of clients seeking him had slowed considerably. Then
too, his time was consumed early on with the building
of Taliesin in Wisconsin. Certainly he would have
welcomed some grand project. He truly needed
money now, with two households to support. There
were still the children and Catherine in Oak Park, and
now with his main studio up north, he also maintained
a small office in Chicago.

In time, two major commissions came his way. One
was for a large entertainment center - a European
style beer-garden - with restaurant, open-air dining, a
stage for musical entertainment. It would consume the
better part of a city block on the south side of the city.

His son John worked on the project with him as the on-site superintending architect. It was near completion of this Midway Gardens job that Wright received the news about the fire at Taliesin and the slaying of his mistress, Mamah, by the deranged servant. He immediately set out for Taliesin, meeting on the train, it is said, Edwin Cheney, who had been apprised of the death of his children.

In the weeks following the tragedy, the devastated Wright received many letters of sympathy, among them one from a stranger that so caught his attention that he responded and eventually met the lady in Chicago. Miriam Noel was to fill the next fourteen years of Wright's life with a relationship that spanned a range from loving solicitude to aggravating harassment.

This time included the period that Wright was occupied almost continually for over five years with the design and construction of the Imperial Hotel in Tokyo, Japan. This commission resulted indirectly from Wright's early-acquired interest in Japanese art, dating back at least to his visit to Japan in 1905, if not to his exposure to it at the 1893 Exposition in Chicago where he undoubtedly saw examples not only of Japanese architecture but of Mayan as well. Allusions to both of those arts are evident in some of his works.

As Japan was becoming more involved in commerce with western countries, the government felt there should be a hotel that conformed to western standards. Through acquaintanceships gained on his visit and after discussions drawn out over several years, Wright got the commission. For five years he spent most of his time in Japan, accompanied by Miriam, while most of the construction was completed. Much of the work was done by hand using primitive and slow procedures. This apparently afforded Wright the time to design nearly everything the hotel would need including furniture, dinnerware, linens, stationery and more. He also had time to design and execute several residences and a girls' school.

Additionally, he was able to expand his collection of Japanese art, some of which he retained and some he sold. Indeed, he became an acknowledged expert in oriental art and functioned as an importer and dealer in Japanese art, a sideline that helped him cope a bit better with the irregular nature of his income.

The Imperial Hotel work kept Wright busy until 1922 when he finally returned to the U. S. for good. His consort, Miriam, became more unstable over the years, her actions exhibiting schizophrenic symptoms. There were arguments between short periods of harmony and Miriam often left for periods of time. Then, in 1923, when Catherine Wright finally secured a divorce some fourteen years after Wright had abandoned his first family, he married Miriam in a midnight ceremony on a bridge near Taliesin. Strangely, the relationship quickly worsened. Within six months she left him, and for the next few years she conducted an aggressive and vitriolic campaign against him.

Upon his return to the States, Wright's professional future was unclear. His Imperial Hotel had regener-ated interest in him and his work, especially when the hotel withstood the ravages of the Great Kanto earthquake, one of Japan's worst, that virtually flattened Tokyo. Wright learned of this good fortune after several days of agony having received early erroneous reports that it had been destroyed.

Among the few substantial buildings that withstood the temblor, Wright's structure came through relatively unscathed. The building had been designed with a "floating foundation" system and with sections and walls that were loosely interconnected, allowing for considerable flexing. The utility and water lines were likewise free to flex within the walls and in separate conduits under the floors. How much these anti-quake techniques contributed to the building's survival is hard to say. It served as one of the main recovery activity centers after the quake devastated the city and left over 150,000 dead.

In spite of whatever accolades this feat generated, Wright was in a low period of production. During his time in Japan, other projects continued to be worked on here at home by his staff operating out of the Taliesin studio. One such commission involved several buildings for the oil heiress and theatrical producer Aline Barnsdall. It was to include a theater in addition to her residence and other structures on a large site below the Hollywood hills in Los Angeles.

With designing and construction coinciding with Wright's full involvement in the Imperial Hotel, supervision was delegated to the Austrian-born architect, R. M. Schindler, with preliminary site preparation and landscaping in the hands of Wright's son Lloyd. Lloyd Wright was initially trained as a landscape architect and had come to California, working first in San Diego. He remained in the Los Angeles area and had an extensive and successful career as an architect. Schindler also remained there and became celebrated for his work, mostly in the International Style.

While only the residence, *Hollyhock House,* and two guest houses were erected, Barnsdall continued to give Wright commissions which, like the theater, were either never begun or never completed. But Wright was not quite through with California.

Wright had first used concrete as the principal material in his 1904 Unity Temple in Oak Park. He used it again, to considerable extent in patterned blocks in the Midway Gardens. And in the Imperial, he used poured reinforced concrete as the support structure covered by a veneer of brick, a local soft stone, and wood. *Hollyhock House* made extensive use of cast concrete as trim and ornament. Now he wanted to show that concrete, the material of gutters and pavements, could constitute the main material for a residence - both exterior and interior walls - and could be used to create decorative effects that otherwise could only be achieved by sculpturing in stone. This he did in four houses in the Los Angeles area as he tried to establish his career anew on the West Coast.

Why Wright referred to them as *textile block* houses is not certain. Was it that the square cast concrete blocks were "knit together" by a mesh of iron bars, or because they were given *texture* with their sculptured surface? Three were built in the hills above Hollywood; one a few miles away in Pasadena.

Lloyd Wright was the on-site superintendent during the roughly two years in which they were erected while Wright was trying to restart his career in Southern California. He may have hoped that the art community (i.e. movie people) would be a fertile field for his advance designs, but this proved to not be the case. Oddly, one can probably find that the homes of the often flamboyant denizens of the movie colony in the 1920s and 30s and even later would likely be labeled as Spanish revival, Mission style, or "ranch style." The folks of the entertainment world turned out to be less adventuresome than some conservative managers and small businessmen that had constituted Wright's Midwestern clientele. Wright eventually retreated to his Taliesin home.

Textile Block
Ennis House, Los Angeles, 1924

4

THE FELLOW/HIP
AND HARD TIME/

Fire seemed to be a recurring nemesis in Wright's life. Long before the devastating and tragic Taliesin fire of 1914, the Wright family came close to suffering a horrible loss. At a Christmastime show in 1903, the two oldest Wright boys and their maternal grand-mother were among those who escaped the disastrous *Iroquois Theater* fire in which over six hundred perished. During his days in Japan, a fire in the hotel where he and Miriam were living threatened his recently acquired valuable collection of Japanese art. Fortunately, she was at hand and able to remove it to safety. But in 1925 Taliesin's living quarters were again ravaged by fire and had to be rebuilt a second time. Wright lost much of his collection in that fire.

Of course, loss of property and lives was a more prevalent danger in those times due to many factors that have since been minimized. In rural areas the dearth of fire fighting equipment rendered buildings subject to total destruction. How many of Wright's buildings were destroyed by fire is probably not known. He was called to restore some after a conflagration had partially destroyed them, like the Moore house built for his attorney friend just down the block from Wright's Oak Park home. After a fire destroyed the entire second floor, Wright rebuilt it making considerable changes in the new version. It is unlikely that an owner could get him to simply redo a house exactly the way it originally was.

But fires fed by combusting oxygen were not the only things blazing in Wright's life in the first years after his return from Japan. At the end of 1924 Olgivanna appeared. She had recently come from Europe with her young daughter and was in process of divorcing her husband. She came from a family of minor aristocrats in Montenegro, which later became a part of Yugoslavia. She had been educated in Russia and had recently lived in France. They met at the ballet in Chicago and Wright quickly courted her. As the new year began, Olgivanna Milanoff was taking Miriam Noel's place at Taliesin. What is more, in December 1925, she gave birth to a baby girl, Iovanna, Wright's seventh child.

Miriam in the meanwhile was continuing her campaign of annoyance. Her flames of fury came in the form of legal assaults aimed at securing some of Wright's assets, as well as verbal and even physical abuse. With the knowledge that another woman was now involved, she multiplied her efforts even to the extent of having Wright arrested and jailed (alleging he was violating the Mann act) when he fled to Minnesota with Olgivanna and the children to avoid her harassments. He was released next day without being charged.

Finally in 1928 a settlement was reached and Wright

and Miriam were divorced. In a short time Olgivanna became the third Mrs. Wright and remained so until her death. The new family of four settled in at Taliesin, but tough times were ahead for them.

If some of the projects that Wright was commissioned to design in the decade of the 1920s had come to fruition, his career would have rebounded quickly and his financial woes might have been solved. But one after another they tumbled by the wayside as clients ran into financial problems. Two resort developments in California failed to materialize. A resort hotel in Arizona was dropped after the stock market crash of October 1929 that ushered in the Great Depression. Few professions suffer more than the architect when the economy is stagnant. Wright was no exception. The Depression stopped virtually all construction in the nation.

With the loss of Taliesin to foreclosure looming, it was Olgivanna's idea to try to form a school of architecture. The tuition fees together with some income from Wright's writings and lectures might save the day - and the farm. This would be an unorthodox school with no formal classes or books. Learning would be achieved by hands-on work and by watching and, undoubtedly, a good deal of listening to *The Master.*

The work was more than just hands-on construction, of which much was done to expand and enhance Taliesin's facilities. It included domestic chores and work in the fields, where most of the food was to be raised. "How can you design a good kitchen if you've never worked in one?" was certainly a logical sounding explanation for having to endure military-style "KP" duty. This is the type of fellowship that the students participated in at the *Frank Lloyd Wright Fellowship*, as the institution was called.

Wright was the sole judge of who was accepted - and who was asked to leave, although Olgivanna may have had much to do with some decisions. There was much in the way of social and cultural events for which Olgivanna was principally responsible. Some students stayed only briefly, others remained much longer. When some commissions eventually materialized, the more experienced and capable students served as superintending architects on the jobs. This communal living and learning had its critics. Even some of Wright's own family likened it to a modified form of slavery. But, for all its idiosyncrasies, the *Fellowship*. did produce, or at least start on their way, a number of competent architects.

The lack of income even caused Wright to work on a project that was commissioned to another. It was the first time since leaving Adler and Sullivan that he was not the principal. He was asked to assist one of his former students in the design of a hotel in Phoenix. Because it was to be of concrete block, Wright was brought on as consulting architect at a flat fee. It seems unlikely that Wright could restrict his involvement on any project to merely consulting on the use of his *textile block* system. For various legal and contractual reasons he undertook the work in this guise, but most experts who have written of the work point with assurance that in its design the Arizona Biltmore Hotel has many unmistakable markings of Wright's hand.

The Biltmore project was one of two that exposed
Wright to what he came to regard as the beauties of
the desert. The other was the depression-doomed
resort at Chandler Arizona, where he had brought out
a small cadre of assistants to begin design and
construction just weeks before the stock market crash
brought an end to the project. They had erected a
camp of temporary shelters in the open desert east of
Phoenix. Some years later, Wright more or less
repeated the experience - this time on his own
account - starting with rough temporary shelters and,
over time, constructed a permanent new headquarters
and called it Taliesin West.

The desert quarters was a winter base to which he
and the *Fellowship* fled before the snows engulfed
Taliesin. In the early days the student body and all the
staff moved in a scattered caravan of vehicles that
included a make shift kitchen - like the "chuck wag-
ons" of the old cattle drives - with Wright in the lead,
driving his Cherokee red Packard touring car. At the
end of the cooler desert months, the trek was done
anew in an easterly direction to Wisconsin. This twice-
yearly relocation continues even today as the students
of the now more formal school split their time between
the two centers. Both Taliesin and Taliesin West
conduct regular daily tours for interested visitors.

Photo by Robert P. Ruschak

Fallingwater
Kaufmann House, Mill Run, PA, 1935

RE/URGE/ICE
- TWO DECADE/ OF GLORY

Wright suffered through a period of seven years when commissions wore almost nonexistent. More time was spent in the expansion of the Taliesin complex than for outside clients. Not only was he financially strapped but his reputation and recognition were dwindling. Many in the profession assumed that his career had come to an end. After all, he would soon reach the age of seventy, which was considered old in those times. But a funny thing happened on Mr. Wright's way to his final days. He managed to squeeze in another two decades of creativity and produced some of his most outstanding work.

A commission came to him through one of the students of the school. The student's father, Edgar Kaufmann Sr., a wealthy merchant, wanted a small weekend retreat built at a site in a heavily wooded mountain area some seventy-five miles southeast of Pittsburgh, Pennsylvania. For many years the Kaufmanns had spent weekends in a small cottage there, enjoying the rugged surroundings where a small stream flowed over giant boulders. Upon viewing the site, Wright decided to place the new building above the waterfall with the tip of the boulder the Kaufman's often sat on to enjoy the stream poking through the living room floor a few feet from the fireplace. With long cantilevered terraces, one above the other, the structure created a stunning visual effect.

The story is told by *Fellowship* students who were there, how Wright "shook the design out of his sleeve," as he used to say, and did it in just a few hours. He was pressed to do so when, after several months, his client phoned from nearby Milwaukee. He wanted to see what progress had been made in the design of the house. Nothing had actually been done - except in Wright's mind. With his students gathered at his drafting table, the Master went to work, producing plan, sections, and elevation drawings. By the time Kaufmann arrived some three to four hours later, he was able to see the design of his little summer retreat that would become one of the most famous, most visited houses in the world.

Now Frank Lloyd Wright was again a name for the art community to pay attention to. Publicity about *Fallingwater* revived his career. A second important commission quickly came to him. He was asked to design the administration building for the S. C. Johnson Wax Company in Racine Wisconsin. The job was quite similar to the earlier Larkin building, an office work place to be located in unsightly industrial surroundings. As in the earlier structure where he placed the windows high on the walls for light but not for sight, here he let light enter through high panels of

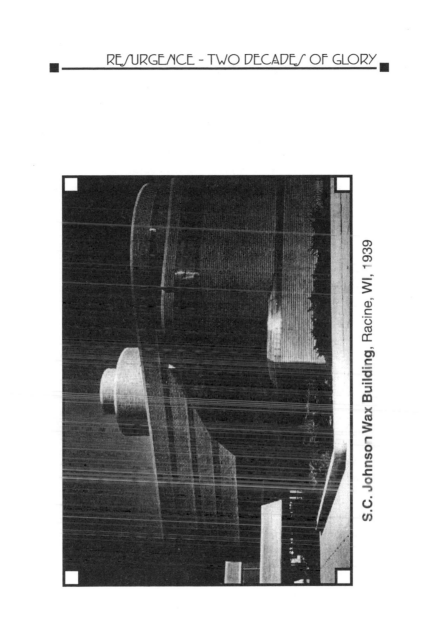

S.C. Johnson Wax Building, Racine, WI, 1939

V.C. Morris Shop, San Francisco, 1948

tubular glass that did not allow outside viewing. Like the Larkin, there would be a large central clerical work area under a high ceiling and surrounded by private office areas on the upper floors which were accessed by balcony-like hallways that overlooked the central atrium .As in the case of *Fallingwater* there is a story - now a legend of sorts - coming out of the construction of the Johnson Wax Building.

Wright had designed an unusual three-story high column to support the roof and ceiling over the expansive central office area. This column was less than a foot in diameter at the floor and tapered out gradually as it rose, then flared out like a large flat flower at the ceiling. Building safety inspectors would not issue permits for its use, afraid it would not support its load. The legendary event, documented by photos and film, came at a demonstration where Wright erected a column, and then, with the skeptical authorities present, loaded it with sand bags and steel beams. It supported many times the weight required before it crumbled. He had designed the interior of the column of steel in a cross-bracing pattern similar to a giant cactus he had studied in the desert. Permission to use the columns was approved.

Just as he had done for the Imperial Hotel, Wright expanded the work here to include the furniture, made of steel in this case, and much in keeping with the *streamline modern* style of the building itself. (Yes, in this case Wright had succumbed to the use of the trendy, corner-rounding style of the thirties and brazenly, shamelessly adopted it as his own.) Nearly ten years later he added the Research Tower in a shape that has an uncanny resemblance to a container in which some of the company's products might be packaged. Like *Fallingwater,* the Johnson Wax Building is open daily for guided tours given to thousands of visitors a year.

In spite of costs that exceed many times Wright's estimates, and in spite of numerous disagreements between Wright and Herbert Johnson, the company president, Johnson commissioned Wright to build the giant *Wingspread* house just outside of Racine, his third major commission in less than two years. Now housing a non-profit foundation established by Johnson, it too can be visited.

These projects must have gone a long way toward ameliorating the financial crisis Wright had been facing. He had almost lost Taliesin to the bank. It was saved with help from a group of friends and former clients who "invested" (if such a term can be used for this venture) in a corporate entity consisting of Wright himself, with its only source of potential income being his future commissions. Thus at the age of seventy Wright was off and running on a new era in his career in which he creates more public buildings and more structures of a grand scale than in his previous fifty years.

Within those two decades scores of residences were also designed and executed. They included his so-called Usonian houses which came the closest to realizing his oft-stated goal of creating a house the typical middle class American family could afford. The first of these was built in 1936 in Madison Wisconsin. These one-floor homes, often in an L-shape plan, were without basement or attic. The "work center" (kitchen/laundry) separated bedrooms from the living-dining area where a space forming an adjunct to the living room replaced the formal dining room, an innovation for that time. It is interesting to note that ten years later as the country worked to solve the post-war housing shortage, homes of this nature were prevalent, and were marketed as *ranch style* homes.

Wright also supplanted the garage with a carport. Usonian houses had radiant heat from heating pipes in the concrete slab floors. Brick, plywood, and glass were the primary construction materials. Wright's idea that his Usonian plan would allow the owner to build it himself, or at least to participate in its construction, depended on the particular skills of the person involved. But Usonians certainly were simplified and a far cry from the Prairie style and any of the huge residences Wright had done earlier.

During his career Wright designed a number of buildings in the skyscraper category (including a mile-high one), but all except one of those projects were the victims of reluctant - perhaps skeptical - potential clients. His one realized high-rise, the Pierce Company Tower in the oil country of eastern Oklahoma, is included in the group of seventeen of his designs specifically honored by the American Institute of Architects. Its main support structure is the central core. The floors are cantilevered out from it to the exterior walls, like branches on a giant fir tree.

Of course, Wright also continued to design houses in individual, non-formatted plans. Now he worked with a variety of forms, including use of the circle, which was conspicuously absent from earlier works. It showed up

Price Company Tower
Bartlesville, OK, 1952

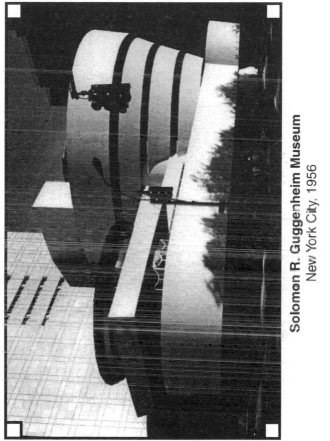

Solomon R. Guggenheim Museum
New York City, 1956

Photo By David Heald

not only in some houses but in his public buildings. A Greek Orthodox church near Milwaukee and the Grady Gammage Memorial Auditorium on the campus of Arizona State University in Tempe are essentially completely circular. Other non-residential buildings included a synagogue, several churches for various Protestant denominations and the design of an entire campus of a Florida college where only eight of the buildings were completed between 1938 and 1954.

Some commercial buildings were also designed and built in the early 1950s, among them a store complex in Beverly Hills, California, and an automobile show-room in New York City. Earlier, Wright had designed the V. C. Morris Gift Shop in San Francisco, with a distinctive three-story high roman brick facade and barrel-like entry. Inside, a cantilevered ramp and balcony circles the shop's walls; a concept he carried over to the Guggenheim Museum design he was then also working on.

By the time he came to design the Guggenheim Museum to take its place on Fifth Avenue in New York City, Wright had also changed his use of concrete. No longer was it to be the cement blocks of the Los Angeles houses or those of the Arizona Biltmore and others of earlier years. Here he utilizes the plasticity of concrete in a circular format. He also uses an old standby of his, the ramp, which he had sometimes used instead of stairs to move people between levels. In the Guggenheim, the art viewer starts at the top and circles around on a gently spiraling incline to the ground floor.

The museum had not yet opened to the public before

Wright died. Other buildings, not as complete but in construction, and some, designed but not yet started, were completed by the staff at Taliesin after his death. Wright's largest executed design is the Marin County Civic Center complex in San Rafael, California consisting of two immense wings containing county offices and courts, joined together at the circular county central library.

When he died in a Phoenix hospital in April 1959 after a brief illness, Wright was just two months shy of his ninety-second birthday. He had been working as usual less than two weeks before. He was buried in the Lloyd Jones' family cemetery not far from Mamah's grave.

Olgivanna continued to oversee the work of the Frank Lloyd Wright Foundation for another quarter century. She died in 1985 and, at her request, Wright's remains were cremated and brought back to Taliesin West and interred beside hers.

**Taliesin West
Scottsdale, Arizona**

APPENDIX

The listings on the next few pages can be useful to the new Wright fan as well as to his more knowledgeable devotees. If a novice, having just breezed though this short text, a little field work is in order. Put your new found knowledge to use, relating the abstract words of the page to the concrete (no pun intended) reality of brick and wood and glass and, yes, concrete. The more advanced enthusiast should do exactly the same.

There are three lists. List "A" gives selected sites in three regions of the country and List "B" names some catalogues or guide books that can direct you to many more Wright-designed structures. I tried to include sites in as wide a spread across the country as possible in the hope you can find one or two reasonably close to home or to where you may frequently travel. List "C" contains titles of some moderately priced books that can increase your knowledge of and stimulate more interest in the works of Frank Lloyd Wright.

Almost all of the listed structures are either public buildings or buildings sometimes open to the public.

You should consult other sources, such as the guide books, or contact a site directly to determine what days and hours they are accessible. Some offer guided tours usually available without prior reservation and lasting 30 to 45 minutes; others allow a self-guided visit. I have omitted some of the more popular sites such as Fallingwater, The Johnson Wax Building, and the two Taliesins where tours may be somewhat longer and some may require reservations. I encourage you to plan a trip to visit these and other popular Wright destinations.

List A - *∫*ITE*∫* TO VI*∫*IT

In the EAST:

Solomon R. Guggenheim Museum
    1071 Fifth Avenue New York, NY

Beth Shalom Synagogue   Old York Rd. at Foxcroft
    Elkins Park, PA   (Philadelphia area)

Isadore J Zimmerman House
    223 Heather St. Manchester, NH

Darwin J. Martin House
    125 Jewett Pkwy. Buffalo, NY

Meyers Medical Clinic
    5441 Fair Hills Ave. Dayton, OH

Florida Southern College (7 campus buildings)
Lakeland, FL

In the MIDWEST

Frederick C. Robby House
5757 S. Woodlawn Ave. Chicago, IL

Rookery Building Lobby
209 S. La Salle St. Chicago, IL

Unity Temple
Lake St. and Kenilworth Ave. Oak Park, IL

Dana-Thomas House
301 E. Lawrence Ave. Springfield, IL

Meyor May House
450 Madison Ave. S. E. Grand Rapids, MI

Annunciation Greek Orthodox Church
North 92nd St. at Congress St. Wauwatosa, WI
(Milwaukee area)

Herbert F. Johnson House (*Wingspread*)
33 E. 4 Mile Rd. Wind Point, WI   (Racine area)

Unitarian Church
900 University Bay Dr. Sherwood Hills, WI
(Madison area)

In the SOUTHWEST

Price Company Tower
   N. E. 6th St. and Dewey Ave. Bartlesville, OK

Dallas Theatre Center (Kalita Humphrys Theater)
   3636 Turtle Creek Blvd. Dallas, TX

Arizona Biltmore Hotel
   Missouri Ave. at 24th St. Phoenix, AZ
   (entrance to hotel/country club complex)

Grady Gammage Memorial Auditorium
   Apache Blvd. at Mill Rd. Tempe, AZ

Anderton Court Shops
   332 N. Rodeo DR. Beverly Hills, CA

Millard House (*La Miniatura*)
   645 Prospect Crescent Pasadena, CA

Kendert Medical Clinic
   1106 Pacific Ave. San Luis Obispo, CA

V. C. Morris Gift Shop
   140 Maiden Lane San Francisco, CA

Marin County Civic Center
   3501 Civic Center Dr. San Rafael, CA
   (East of route US101
      at North San Pedro Rd. exit.)

List B - GUIDE BOOKS

FRANK LLOYD WRIGHT FIELD GUIDE - METROCHICAGO
Thomas Heinz   Academy Editions (UK)
ISBN 047197692X

FINDING THE WRIGHT PLACES IN CALIFORNIA AND ARIZONA
H. J. Michel   One Palm Books
ISBN 0-9652237-3-6
(Maps, directions to sites and vignettes of Wright's life.)

WRIGHT SITES, A Guide to
Frank Lloyd Wright Public Places
A.Sanderson, Ed. Princeton Architectural Press
ISBN 1-56898-041 8

THE ARCHITECTURE OF FRANK LLOYD WRIGHT,
A Complete Catalog Second Edition
William Allin Storrer The MIT Press
ISBN 026269080-2

List C - /UGGE/TED READING

Birk, Melanie. *Frank Lloyd Wright and the Prairie.*
Universal Publishing, Inc. 1998
ISBN 0789301407

Boulton, Alexander. *Frank Lloyd Wright: Architect*
- an Illustrated Biography.
Rizzoli International. 1993
ISBN 0847816834

Hoppen, David W.
The Seven Ages of Frank Lloyd Wright.
Dover Publications, Inc. 1997   ISBN 048629420X

McDonough, Yona Z. *Frank Lloyd Wright.*
Chelsea House Publishers. 1992
ISBN 0791016269

Smith, Kathryn. *Frank Lloyd Wright*
- America's Master Architect.
Abbeyville Press, Inc. 1998
ISBN 0789202875

Tafel, Edgar. *About Wright - An Album of Recollections*
By Those Who Knew Frank Lloyd Wright
John Wiley and Sons, Inc.
ISBN 0471119237

Wright, John Lloyd. *My Father, Frank Lloyd Wright*
Dover Publications, Inc. 1992
ISBN 0486269868

PHOTO CREDITS
AND ACKNOWLEDGEMENT

The author is grateful to the organizations listed here for the photographs on the pages indicated, provided through their courtesy.

p.

36 - The Trust for Preservation of Cultural Heritage, *Ennis-Brown House*, Los Angeles, CA; (p. 36; back cover background design)

42- *Fallingwater*, Photo by Robert P. Ruschak courtesy of The Western Pennsylvania Conservancy, Mill Run, PA

45 - S. C. Johnson Wax Company, Racine, WI

50 - Bartlesville Convention and Visitors Bureau, Bartlesville, OK

51 - © The Solomon R. Guggenheim Foundation, New York, NY; Photo by David Heald.

Cultural Affairs Dept., City of Los Angeles (*Hollyhock House* art glass detail; front cover background design)

All other photographs are by the author.

INDEX

Oak Park, IL, Home, 23;
  life in, 11, 23-24, 28
Price Company Tower, 49-50
Prairie Houses, 12, 15-16
Robie House, 14

Silsbee, Joseph, 21, 23
skyscrapers, 10, 49
Sullivan, Louis H.
  (Alder & Sullivan)
  10-12, 21
Taliesin, Wis. 29, 31, 37, 43;
  West, 41,54
Textile blocks, 35, 40
Unity Temple, 15-16, 24, 35
Usonian houses, 48-49

Wright, Anna (mother)
  17-18, 22
Wright, Catherine (Tobin)
  22, 24, 27-28, 31, 33

Wright, Frank Lloyd,
  Apprenticeship, 10-11, 21;
  attire of, 22, 25;
  automobiles of, 24-25, 41;
  birth, 17;
  Chicago, move to, 20-21;
  childhood stories of, 20-21;
  death of, 53;
  divorces, 33,38;
  draftsman, as a, 10;
  early fame, 15;
  education of, 9, 10;
  ego of, 16, 27;
  Europe in, 16, 27-28, 31;
  leaves Sullivan, 12;